A CHRISTMAS STORY
with St. Joseph

BY GERALDINE GUADAGNO

ILLUSTRATED BY MARIA CRISTINA LO CASCIO

4

God had special plans for Joseph.

When Joseph was a boy, his father taught him how to work and how to pray.

Joseph learned to choose sturdy wood. He learned to measure it, cut it with saws, and nail it together. He practiced again and again. Soon he could use his tools without cutting his fingers. He could make the wood so smooth that he did not get splinters.

Joseph also learned to pray the psalms. He learned to follow God's laws, the Ten Commandments, which God had given to Moses. He learned to love God with all his mind and all his heart and all his strength.

"Help me to do the things that are good and kind," Joseph prayed. And God helped him. Joseph grew up to be a good, kind man with a carpenter's hands that he used to work and to pray.

7

When Joseph was grown, he met a young woman named Mary. He offered her his hands, hard and rough from good, honest work. They were strong but gentle hands. He wanted to use them to care for Mary. Her family was pleased, and Joseph and Mary planned the day when they could be married.

9

A little while before their wedding, Mary came to Joseph.

"Joseph," she said, "I'm going to have a baby."

Joseph was confused and troubled. He had always wanted to please God and do what was right. He loved Mary and wanted her to be his wife. He would do nothing to hurt or harm her. But how could there be a baby?

II

When Joseph was alone, he did what he always did when he was confused and troubled. He put his hands together, and he prayed.

"Father God," he said, "what should I do? How can I do what is right and good?"

Joseph felt very tired. He was still thinking about Mary and her baby when he fell asleep.

God answered Joseph's prayers. Joseph dreamed. And in his
dream, he saw an angel who gave him a message from God.

"Don't be afraid, Joseph. Mary is good and kind. She
has done nothing wrong. God wants you to marry her and
look after her. Mary's child is from the Holy Spirit. She will
have a Son, and you will call him Jesus."

15

When Joseph woke up, he knew that God had spoken to him.
He understood that Mary's baby was very special and that he,
Joseph, had been given a special job to do.

Joseph took Mary home as his wife. Together they prepared
for the birth of her baby, the baby they would call Jesus.

17

Some months later, the Roman emperor decided that there would be a census of all his people. Everyone had to return to the home of their ancestors to be counted.

Joseph was a descendant of King David, so he and Mary had to go to Bethlehem, a journey of several days. Hand in hand they traveled with many others along dusty roads.

19

When they arrived in Bethlehem, Joseph knocked firmly on door after door. He hoped to find a room, a place where they could stay after their journey.

Then Mary said to Joseph, "I think the baby is coming tonight."

21

*I*t was a starry night when Joseph found a stable. He placed clean hay in the manger to make ready a place for Mary's baby

Joseph stayed with Mary until finally God's Son, Jesus, the promised Savior, was born. He held the baby with hands as strong and gentle and tender as any father's hands.

Joseph prayed again:

"Father God, now more than ever, help me to do what is right and good for this holy, precious child."

23

Mary and Joseph did not get much sleep that night. Shepherds came to visit who had already heard of the baby's birth.

They had been tending their sheep on a hillside when suddenly an angel appeared. "Don't be afraid," the angel had said. "A Savior has been born. You'll find him in a manger." Then there was a host of angels. The echoes of the angels' song seemed to come with the shepherds to Bethlehem:

"Glory to God in the highest and peace to all people on earth!"

On another starry night, Joseph watched in wonder as camels stopped outside the door of their little house in Bethlehem. Wise men entered, bringing gifts for Jesus, whom they called a baby King.

Joseph saw the men kneel and worship the child he helped care for. When they left, he held in his hands the gifts they had left— gold, frankincense, and myrrh—and put them safely away.

That night God sent his angel to Joseph in another dream.

"Take the child and his mother to Egypt, for Herod plans to kill him! Stay there until I tell you it is safe to return."

Joseph protected Mary and Jesus as they left Bethlehem by night and traveled to Egypt. Joseph provided them with food, shelter, and safety while they made their home in a foreign land until God sent his angel in a third dream.

"Return to Israel, Joseph. The people who were seeking the child's life are dead."

Joseph took Mary and Jesus to Israel and to a home in Nazareth where, just like his own father, Joseph taught Jesus how to work and how to pray.

Joseph, Mary, and Jesus were all safely in God's hands.

First published in 2010
as St. Joseph's Story

Copyright © 2010 Anno Domini Publishing
www.ad-publishing.com
Text copyright © 2010 Geraldine Guadagno
Illustrations copyright © 2010 Maria Cristina Lo Cascio
All rights reserved

A Christmas Story with St. Joseph
Copyright © 2017
Published in the U.S. and Canada by
The Word Among Us Press
7115 Guilford Drive, Suite 100
Frederick, MD 21704, USA
www.wau.org

ISBN: 978-1-59325-322-6

Publishing Director: Annette Reynolds
Art Director: Gerald Rogers
Pre-production Manager: Doug Hewitt

Printed and bound in Malaysia
July 2017